Printed in the United States
By Bookmasters

POEMS *of* HOPE

INSPIRATION
ANIMATE-INSPIRE

KING IVES

WESTBOW
PRESS®
A DIVISION OF THOMAS NELSON
& ZONDERVAN

WestBow Press books may be ordered through booksellers or by contacting:

WestBow Press
A Division of Thomas Nelson & Zondervan
1663 Liberty Drive
Bloomington, IN 47403
www.westbowpress.com
1 (866) 928-1240

ISBN: 978-1-5127-8079-6 (sc)
ISBN: 978-1-5127-8545-6 (e)

Print information available on the last page.

WestBow Press rev. date: 04/18/2017

Contents

A COWBOY'S PRAYER

Riding long dusty trail early dawn setting sun alone horse I tired want to quit all I can bear out of nowhere voice speaks heart scene majestic beauty far as eye can see a cowboy's prayer.

Cowboy's life hard ask self when most happy under starring skies old faithful and I together over seer not seen natural eye heart Master confidant guide troubles bare a cowboy's prayer.

Night fall bedded down fire bright book doesn't have fancy pictures like most just plain writing life all that's pure Holy Rembrandt of majestic beauty heaven earth mystery mortal eye yet power over life death inner even a cowboy's prayer.

A DAY OF HOPE AND DREAMS

911 a day of hope dreams blink of an eye nothing would ever be the same.

Heart's as a nation filled of sadness their hopes dreams will live of us by stopping all madness.

On that day words couldn't express what we felt as if heart would melt.

To their love one's and to the people as a nation their bravery inner will live of infamy by our action deed words we say of God's Grace mercy America will pave way all nations brighter day.

As we approach each new days dawn tell love one's how much we love them thank God for his mercy Grace Life is like a hour glass filled of sand know not what hour it will take us by hand.

A FIELD TO GROW IN

World sorrow woe heart seed sown solid foundation free a field to grow in.

Heart heavy laden mortal body flesh, clay temptation things world breathe Grace Mercy a field to grow in.

Bodies out of control hate envy heart a field to grow in.

World filled temptation Holy Spirit holds fast pray heart longing to mend a field to grow in.

Each day look can't score mind's pondering rushing flow lost of that only see that can't see only then a field to grow in.

ALONE FORSAKEN

Heart despair life tossed taken alone forsaken.

Life ripping scale balance reason shaken alone forsaken.

Hope desire whirl wind sand life shuffle ruffle heart awaken alone forsaken.

Adult life decisions mind control console heart shaken alone forsaken.

Upon knee pray sin for given taken alone forsaken.

Night fall day bed wall bare emptiness inner body aching mercies Grace Inner awaken alone forsaken.

ANGEL

Child innocent gift God entrusted earthly parent's console, love, hold angel.

Heart passion sacrifice humbled Spirit life angel.

Bow head knee reverence day tongue wisdom this body clay angel.

Stretch forth hand all of need go that extra mile only a while mother, father wisdom

Honor knowledge without rage angel.

Heart resting peace angel of death awaits inner angel.

BLUE MOON

Heart lonely torn apart down out life gloom blue moon.

Eye's world heart empty misery frolic mortal flesh doom blue moon.

Song bird lullaby song music ear croon blue moon.

Tempt not fate journey's end loom blue moon.

Gentle breeze body old weak alone rose garden after noon blue moon.

Youth no longer see reminisce what use to be flower radiant imminent bloom blue moon.

BROKEN PROMISE

Have capacity care if not wisdom lost within to share broken promise.

Life solid heart hollow without heart can't lead follow broken promise.

Inner once of solid foundation folded double minded broken promise.

Cheat lie reason without why grumble broken promise.

To turn back one of need inner lost reap grumble broken promise.

World sin heart mend journey's end judge not ones destiny hand without faith Grace broken promise.

BUTTER FLIES, MORNING WILD FLOWERS, AND AFTER-NOON

When two lip's meet heart in twine love coursing mortal flesh heart recall by gone day's heart croon butter flies, morning wild flowers, and after-noon.

Hands locked together passion love sandy beach lighted moon butter flies, morning wild flowers, and after-noon.

Life present's many favors' far near within inner heart heavenly tunes butter flies, morning wild flowers, and after-noon.

Love splendid creation inner heart God hold love butter flies, morning wild flowers, and after-noon.

CAROLINA MOON

Porch starring sky beauty glow heart croon Carolina moon.

Light by night guide way heart bay soul stray peace stay burdens bare eyes bloom Carolina moon.

Bed time kneel pray his will day room dark imagination looms heart peace wed soon Carolina moon.

To stand upon sand ocean's water serene still beauty man holding brush tear all he had to pay we stand afternoon under Carolina moon.

Walk of faith day help brother along way light shine beauty as of his light sent down Carolina moon.

Moon's glow beaming rose breathe fragrance passing by patience soon Carolina moon.

CHILD BENEATH MASTER'S FEET

Early dawn baby born feet tiny small mom dad ten foot tall.

He gave us joy laughter through the years eyes watered fear mom dad dried tear.

Child teen's man liked by all means.

He adored body building martial art heart.

A body bench pressing four hundred pounds heart child mild Spirit humbled compassionate Nile.

Brother's, Sister's adore smiles galore sleeping Jesus golden shore.

Young man thirty slept heart gold angel of death touched inner God's hand hold.

His presences we'll miss heart bliss God's Grace Mercy endure heal awaiting thy season endless sleep child beneath Master's feet.

Son peace sleep weeps no more mom dad heavenly moon hand hold soon child beneath Master's feet.

COFFEE IN THE MORNING

Early dawn feet floor headed door steaming cup liquid solid black sip coffee in the morning.

Black steaming spout fragrance fine divine coffee in the morning.

Bone chilled trembling lip partake black gold black as night yet warmth soothing inner will coffee in the morning.

Dinner laid quarter down spent it a round got to have it know that cup called job coffee in the morning.

Awaken sleep cup black gold pain eased bones warm let's go job coffee in the morning.

As we sat drank cup after cup liquid black piping hot reality mercy Grace Seed called job coffee in the morning.

CHRISTMAS

Early dawn snow covered ground icicles pointed round Christmas.

Eye's stare fog hovering pond water blue Smokey mountain morning serene still Christmas.

Body old compassion hold inner actions speak peace compassion heart achieve console Christmas.

Tree green cedar ornaments bells bows icicles candy cane fragrance savor air ham ice cream children dream angel tree adore special occasion JESUS birth night savior came earth Christmas.

COW-BOY

Riding range all day blue sky wind upon bone beauty hold cattle lowing sun glowing peace joy hold cow-boy.

Equine grazing grass ankle deep magnificent structure molded creator body Spirit joy cow-boy.

Coyotes howling beneath moon beneath stars bright friends' gone emptiness heart alone destiny hold cow-boy.

Early dawn setting sun cattle roping branding camp fire spinning yarns companion horse dream roam experience nature's majestic beauty all it has to hold life only God controls cow-boy.

DREAMS COMING TRUE

Dream blessings seen heart dreams coming true.

Wandering, blue knee meek lowly dreams coming true.

Struggle life stumble grumble without clue Master heart dreams coming true.

Body tired age creeping by pondering why upon knee humble of thee dreams coming true.

Life fear heart meek lowly Bible fruit inner dreams coming true.

Life love heart inner claim our dues dreams coming true.

DRIFTER

Traveling highway tired old, lonely drifter.

Inner lost without control no one hold alone heart whirl drifter.

Tomorrow new day prayed sins away this night I'm to leave heart not grieve drifter.

I see things during day seem far away mortal flesh kneel pray safe harm heart not alarmed drifter.

Family ties once enjoyed gone must it is eye to see sorrow grief mortal flesh inner beauty hold drifter.

Cold doctor nature friend sun shines this body clay traveling pilgrim drifter.

FALLEN ANGEL

Mortal body flesh endure heal kneel fallen angel.

Wrath oneself lust greed heeds fallen angel.

Envy fault other's without thought self Spirit lost price fallen angel.

Mountain's climbed lost self inner book told fallen angel.

Win gain unable to contemplate reality abundance lost heart complain blame fallen angel.

Life strife agony hold double minded body soul toss turn unable beauty rose fallen angel.

Body tired feeble old disease hold unable to console mold fallen angel.

FLOWER

Fragrance air beauty compare flower.
Beauty love enduring life hope flower.
Heartbroken mortal flesh scorned yet something small light heart flower.
Rose's covered field innocence beauty flower.

FOOL'S PARADISE

Mind waste reality face heart fool's paradise.

Life protest haste not knowing best mangled deceived fool's paradise.

Rush no thought day heart lost fool's paradise.

Mind anger inner lost fool's paradise.

Young restless now then no thought when Grace Fall no thought calling stalling fool's paradise

Heart cold tongue scold heart bold lost meekness inner beauty no longer hold fool's paradise.

Take hand oh Lord Day night cleanse inner impurities heart light shine wisdom depart fool's paradise.

FREE AT LAST

Inner lost life no meaning heart defeated shame inner fast free at last.
Longing rest mortal body flesh live die free at last.
Life's burden bare rose humble, lowly, mild, sun flower heart free at last.
Weep not life heart flower beauty freshness duty calling free at last.
Old feeble tired body worn mercy Lord Walk of thee thy wraths free at last.

GOD'S EYE

Sigh hide all God's eye.

Passing world wisdom untaught love passed by God's eye.

Mercy Grace lost without run hide God's eye.

Eye tear inner without fear Spirit lost heart cry God's eye.

Inner vapor dew mists I God's eye.

Autumn leaves vibrant color majestic beauty mercy Grace Lie God's eye.

GOD'S RAIN BOW

Heaven's blue sky beauty mystery glow God's rain bow.

Beneath sunned blue sky water flow mortal flesh bide life God's rain bow.

Stillness night stars bright mortal beauty behold God's rain bow.

Foot stool throne dine of me eternity grow God's rain bow.

Beauty art nature mystery canvas painted back ground gold God's rain bow.

GOD'S THRONE

Birth death whence born God's throne.

Life not ours to hold borrow things not ours to own God's throne.

Fertilize ground crop nigh heat sigh prayer faith hand worn God's throne.

Spring flowers beauty adore mercy Grace known God's throne.

Glass water book butter fly rose fragrance nectar nose mercy Grace Seed sown God's throne.

GLORY

Mortal flesh slip fall Grace Sit right hand father bold Glory.

Gave his best skies darkened back turned let go that we rest only begotten son death everlasting life hold Glory.

Why father tempted tried tormented Satan defeated light Glory.

Body old feeble hand tender warm inner beauty hold mold Glory.

Alpha Omega beginning ending gold Glory too have and to hold eternity.

GREELEYVILLE HIGH SCHOOL LEGEND LIVE ON

Days gone by building wood concrete brick hallowed hall could talk no one fault. Memories embedded time hopes dreams achievements men women walked the walk talked the talk Greeley-Ville High School faded Glory left story legends course set history inner reached out touched clouds foam Greeley-Ville High School home. School fought candy bought books sought each a dream to be all they could be these Greeley-Ville High School legends sailed Land Sea.

Greeley-Ville High School mascot Tiger colors red white blue beginning ending class C school of its day Hartsville Relay went no C school dared trod call Greeley-Ville High School tall.

Last graduating class Greeley-Ville High School nine only could go back time men women legends of time will write their names pages of history held Greeley-Ville High School exalted of standard.

Years past lost contact but few renew.

Of mind fellow class mates Owen Pack David McKnight Owen called big O track base-ball basket-ball foot-ball gentle giant gave all.

David McKnight ran mile with ease pleased State Track Meet Columbia, S. C. legends seekers takers history makers.

Years passed think of all the women men before us that held Greeley-Ville High School exalted of honor will live on of heart mind legends seekers history makers. Of self no words record stands of its self.

HARVEST MOON

Stars bright sky golden circle guiding night soon harvest moon.

Light shine inner heart hold beauty loom harvest moon.

Old man brush shoulder lighting night beauty serene still canvas painted portrait eye behold afternoon harvest moon.

Early morning give thanks' day guide hand all that I touch setting sun bloom harvest moon.

HE CALLED MY NAME

Morning night stillness peace mortal body fleshes same he called my name.
Sun shine blue sky beauty mystery hold heart without blame he called my name.
Humble is he eye not see love endures heartache pain comfort abide without pride
upon knee came he called my name.
Drifting place to place flowing water tide nowhere to hide alone forsaken end of road
all said done body tired lame he called my name.

HE IS RISEN

Born Bethlehem child savoir Christmas night able he is risen.
Jew's God's chosen people sent only begotten son die cross gentiles not cry
guaranteed place heaven he is risen.
Defeated death grave all walk Grace solid sound he is risen.
Set right hand father intermediate Jesus we enjoy eternal life without strife heaven he
is risen.

HOPE

What are people to become without intellect lost emptiness only of intellect dreams contemplates hope.

Contemplate mind inner can't be seen natural eye dreams destiny expectations hope.

Heart burning endeavor partake confide God harvest destiny dreams hope.

Lives passing by dismay heart heavy laden empty contemplate all lost only God's Grace Mercy heart hope.

Dust of ground formed air breathed nostril back to dust whence came breathe taken creator author finisher life hope.

Early dawn setting sun thanks all done this body clay molded image without any books written no songs sing a music creator author finisher boss destiny dream hope.

IT'S CHRISTMAS

Early morning fog canvas painted landscape serene still nature inner it's Christmas.
Stars bright golden moon night guided light mystery mortal man contemplates reality
Holy Spirit its Christmas.
Search heart daily before we speak not to offend judge not that we be judged
journey's end savor air fragrances passed down above love it's Christmas.
Crystal blue water fish lily pads colors galore sun's golden ray's warm flesh natures
gift appreciate rest its Christmas.
Pity patter little feet floor laughing crying joyous sounds galore gift entrusted earthly
parent's to love hold console joy they bring young old three hundred sixty five days a
year little ones love innocent pure as a dove God's eye it's Christmas.
Star manger stable Bethlehem gift's bought wise men there be life after death all who
endure humbleness love peace God's birth it's Christmas.

KINGDOM

Heaven mystery eye beauty beholds not yet seen God's majestic beauty mercy Grace Kingdom.

Leaves blowing wind different color shape size heart peace lay kingdom.

Water clear as crystal flowing stream beauty beholds heart inner is kingdom.

Sun shining grass golden waves crystal chandelier kingdom.

Heat day coolness night mortal flesh inner heaven earth unfold kingdom.

LACY AND I

Lacy red white blaze blond mane tail together as one trail canvas painted portrait beauty serene still Lacy and I trail.
Lacy gentle as a butter fly friend companion side by side ride gentle breeze flowers pass by beneath God's blue sky Grace Lacy and I.

LAST HOUR

Time place due season things told reason love peace inner hold heart gentle flower last hour.

Body tired life scorned heart gentle inner transformed Journey end God's tower last hour.

Twinkling eye life mist vapor dew know not hour fate hand God's tower last hour.

Life taken world things blame inner peace joy love hold image power last hour.

Rising dawn setting sun bodily flesh contemplate reality sign his coming earth free last hour.

LILLIES OF THE FIELD

Flower majestic beauty real lilies of the field.

Natures beauty peace love inner heal lilies of the field.

Art nature's beauties enjoy hold tranquil inner tranquility kneel lilies of the field.

Field bursting of color fragrance beyond compare life spinning wheel reality simplicity feel lilies of the field.

LILY PAD

Peace contentment nature's beauty serene still frogs croaking lily pad.
Beautiful green pads water blue comfort heart love once had lily pad.
Waiting nature's creatures amid lustrous green foliage lullaby glad lily pad.
Beside water still vegetation life art frogs croaking of harmony thick green cushions comfort lily pad.

LILY PAD WALTZ

Afternoon sit watching frog's croaking peace inner life all not sad lily pad waltz.
Greenish pads big round floating water tide wind by side moment times had lily pad
waltz.
Lonely inner lost no one console water lily pad breath taking beauty eye behold
moment time lad lily pad waltz.
Water's tide serene still lily pad peace joy instill time youth mom dad lily pad waltz.

LONELY IS THE HEART

Body tired rejected life can't escape strife mortal flesh falling apart lonely is the heart.
Deceitful mind tangled vine connive envy those meet hate can't relate lost without wisdom knowledge mate lonely is the heart.
Search things no acclaim blame lose touch reality drift wood sand intelligent smart lonely is the heart.
Contemplate universe all it has to offer mortal flesh power lost inner art lonely is the heart.

LONGING OF NIGHT

Morning glory beauty charm life hustle bustle strife mortal flesh blight longing of night.

Inner blight day temptation world inner lost of flight longing of night.

Run plays enjoy life inner bright longing of night.

Moon awaits night stars bright light glowing earth night inner longing of night.

Sky falling star peace love compassion mystery beauty Glory sight longing of night.

Heaven pain no more home joy laughter serene still heart meek lowly without flight longing of night.

LORD HOLD ME WHILE I CRY

Born to die contemplate why life try Lord hold me while I cry.
Sorrow heart ache pain blame lives gone due season world good bye Lord hold me while I cry.
Life struggle achieve believe yet grieve mortal body flesh toss turn soul yearn tangled vine deceive lie Lord hold me while I cry.
Early dawn majestic beauty contemplate how can it be only of heart Spirit realm of aesthetics mystery solved no longer sigh Lord hold me while I cry.
Mortal body scorn torn world disdain mercy Grace heart empty without place separate heart world mercy Grace faith without Holy Spirit cream without pie Lord hold me while I cry.

LOST PEARL

Inner drift like water roaring sea snow capped waves whirl lost pearl.

Road twist turn mountain grass green wind echoes curve lost pearl.

Water crystal blue pure diamonds glitter lost pearl.

Flower honey dew beauty unfolds natures gift hold lost pearl.

Eye world Mother Nature failed heart contemplates why reality lost pearl.

MORNING PRAYER

As I awake early morn freshness invigorating fragrance everywhere Morning Prayer.
Dawn kneel pray quietness serene still no one knows where Master I Morning Prayer.
Early dawn beauty Glory old feeble heart Master bare Morning Prayer.
Day night knee pray teacher healer trials bare Master there Morning Prayer.

NO ONE LIKE YOU

Good morning Jesus how are you today inner tired renew no one like you.
Fleshly body your image sin family friends try to fit in no one like you.
A body can run so far not up to par mercy Grace morning dew no one like you.
Life rush no thought time eternity step away let not morning noon sun down pass I
not call true no one like you.

PLAT-FORM

Birth adult hood image looked upon regardless whence born plat form.

Flowers blooming of May beauty eye bay pray plat form.

Heart gentle hope love compassion those scorned owned plat form.

No matter how far life traveled avail young old new born plat form.

Brutalize image bestowed inner higher power moral character eye vigilant church leader ship home plate plat form.

Youth old age honesty dignity love compassion generosity friend to end no matter when solid foundation plat form.

ROSES BY SEA

Strolling ocean moon light fragrance air refine divine majestic beauty savor see roses by sea.

Canvas painted portrait vision freshen inner soothing as tea roses by sea.

Petals velvet color sparkling night everlasting gift light only of him be roses by sea.

Painted portrait not by mortal man picture life other side moon lighting nature divine only he can fold unfold seasoning reasoning meekness lowly peace joy all free roses by sea.

SLIDING ON AN ICE OF FROZEN DREAMS

Heartache pain slip fall inner contemplate life silence screams quit sliding on an ice of frozen dreams.

Early dawn sun set peace beyond all understanding mortal flesh sacred exalt peace love compassion beauty contemplate no longer sliding on an ice of frozen dreams.

Life blessing beyond compare savor all it has to offer inner beam dissipate sliding on an ice of frozen dreams.

Mortal thirst life decay lusting things world inner light, merriment hearts pass sliding on an ice of frozen dreams.

In the event of tragedy that struck a nation healing a nation divided all are created equally regardless race origin took nine inner's his finest to bring unity love peace beyond all understanding that those nine inner's live of our heart mind Spirit of them we live of unity love peace no longer sliding on an ice of frozen dreams.

Let every day be a reminder what it took to bring America together as a nation of one under God liberty justice for all that we as a nation no longer sliding on an ice of frozen dreams.

Every flower lake river tree green meadow sky eyes exalt God's beauty mercy Grace no longer sliding on an ice of frozen dreams.

Help thy brother sister along kind word say reach out those of need heart light hope those of despair together as a nation undivided honoring those nine inner's that displayed exaltation of peace love mercy exalted of beauty Grace no longer sliding on an ice of frozen dreams.

SONG BIRD

Early dawn sun golden round sound heard song bird.

Creatures innocent of God different shapes capabilities small yet mighty gift beauty word song bird.

Work play lark sky power free strength gird song bird.

Heart fear tears sweet God's choir heard song bird.

Place beyond mortal reality no pain blame free as morning dew raised song bird.

Come dine table rest life eternal music harp golden voice lark song bird.

STILLNESS OF NIGHT

Moon gold sky crystal black char coal summer breeze skin eyes gaze stars light stillness of night.

Heart humble lowly night black cold mortal body flesh inner pondering flight stillness of night.

Sky crystal black magic scented pine fragrance nose heart humble, right rose stillness of night.

Moon gold angel inner awaiting beauty unfolds stillness of night.

SOUTH CAROLINA IN THE MORNING

Early dawn fog pond heart safe harm freshness air early dawn Grace South Carolina in the morning.

Night open door early dawn robin red breast tree mercy Grace see natures art gift duteous heart Grace South Carolina in the morning.

Early dawn flowers bloom God's creatures partake nectar womb mortal flesh breathe fragrance early dawn Grace South Carolina in the morning.

Ice crystal chandler beauty unfolds early dawn Grace South Carolina in the morning.

Bed kneel pray early dawn sun blue sky clouds white picture reality early dawn Grace South Carolina in the morning.

STRAW BERRY ROAN

Four legged friend made of Spirit nature strength beauty hold born strawberry roan.
Watch gallop land magnificent Spirit coat shiny softness silk adorn strawberry roan.
My friend to the end my guide helping hand miles to gather roam love that
strawberry roan.
Answer call summer winter fall back all task not complain moan strawberry roan.
Rides over land water plain majestic beauty strength color endurance gift nature
canvas painted portrait fully grown strawberry roan.

SUGAR CANE

Brown stalks large round tall sweet brown sugar field olden time fame sugar cane.

Molasses sweet gift nature nectar heavenly divine God's love rain sugar cane.

Stalks green blades sharp foliage fame sugar cane.

Breakfast syrup poured over pan cakes dark sticky surface bursting of sweetness enchantment tasty as its candy counter part Mary Jane sugar cane.

Once dried whittle bend any shape form fishing pole hold decorated stalks notched of beauty untamed sugar cane.

SUMMER ROSE

Spring flower nigh heart sigh early dawn dew heart lowly mild gold summer rose.
Early dawn golden sun nature art eyes have not seen only inner exalt beauty flower
hold summer rose.
Sun blue sky flower kissed morning dew pedals soft as silk God hold love told
summer rose.
Nature beauty earthly shore eye closed heart lost comprehend beauty summer rose.

SUN SET SERENADE

Late afternoon sun at bay canvas painted portrait beauty sun set serenade.
Sky sun golden round heaven glow fade mystery is sun set serenade.
Dust ground came back dust ground gain no one blame roses bloom inner mystery
mortal flesh earth made laid sun set serenade.
Before dark sky turns pink after rain colors engrave circle majestic beauty inner
rainbow power sun set serenade.

THE CALL

Heart render me meek lowly humble Spirit tall the call.

Eyes blessed light night guide burden hall the call.

Tempted tried patience cried peers stead fast pray I not fall the call.

Sweet dreams sleep God's arm complete destiny achieved believed hallowed hall the call.

Walk of me daily stay speaks softly bosom soil not inner the call.

Journey's end bend inner no more mend task completed deleted cross wall the call.

THE MOMENT

Time place essence of life let go temptation burden strife within inner joy comfort peace hold the moment.

Life disappointment pass our way be not dismayed portrayed as less likely eyes of others innovate inner partake what's good pure truth light the moment.

Captivate inner concept life deep within inner mortal flesh set free weight emptiness the moment.

Fast pace life nerves up roar no time self life's hustle bustles nowhere to go heart faint stop savor time beauty store search inner beauty unlock door the moment.

Surrounded art beauty serene still canvas covered portrait gold times place serenity unfolds hold the moment.

THESE HANDS

It's not hard ships we share but quantity time with others helping achieve believe heart rest not grieve together as one band these hands.

Hands calloused aged time journey ending calling all partake part what's right reasonable God's likeness stand these hands.

Give strength as I bare burden raft ability gift talent bestowed to walk Holy your foot stool sand these hands.

Come of me see beauty in all its splendor weep not work well done hands calloused aged time answered call without bias these hands.

Rose early dawn hands of warmth, compassion, love heart meek lowly those with without friend young old air land these hands.

UNFOLDING ROSE

Rose tiny flower God's design who am I to unfold art beauty land unfolding rose.
Unfold rose hand rose die only God can rose unfold beauty Grace Petal soft mystery
life unfolding rose.
Rose many colors bloom bride waiting groom am I to unfold rose without knowledge
life unfolding rose.
Trust God daily heart obey truth say knee's pray God is of me each step weigh
unfolding rose.
Inner fate heavenly father knows clothes bone left confident new body revealed as
only he knows unfolding rose.

UNTO THY GLORY

Earth mortal flesh made breath breathed nostril life unto thy glory.

Hope faith blessed he of peace inner welcome unto thy glory.

Body old feeble eyes glazed heart inner hold unto thy glory.

Weep not I'm not far away morning dew sun golden round rose hold mold unto thy glory.

Keep not away thy duties golden shore feet light run play milk honey day dues paid heaven stay angel's wings soar unto thy glory.

WE SPEAK YOUR NAME

Once child now grown what vision compassion you bring word song purity heart you came we speak your name.

You up lifted the strong weak words spoke truth honor left hope dreams pride without envy blame we speak your name.

Early dawn setting sun beauty art words actions deeds Glory fame we speak your name.

Child console heart compassionate gave encouragement faith hope despair you were there life's game we speak your name.

Without thought fame reached out those less fortunate gave time self heart eyes starred unseen beauty rose eternity without blemish pain we speak your name.

Chartered course destiny answered call stood tall world left legacy words beautifully phrased poetically stated appreciation art song reminder not where we came from or where we been reality mortal flesh same we speak your name.

WALK INTO TOMORROW

Head bowed eyes hazed Grace Walk into tomorrow.

Cherish that not seen Grace I walk into tomorrow.

Anger inner abomination fear without love can't walk into tomorrow.

Eye exalts beauty only God can give wisdom heart walk into tomorrow.

Be of a solid foundation truth love faith hope walk into tomorrow.

WHISPERING PINE

Alone peace time fragrance so fine whispering pine.

Straw so green peace mind whispering pine.

Tree big round bark brown ground mortal flesh dust turmoil line whispering pine.

Beneath pine fragrance time birds chirp vine whispering pine.

Breezes face gift ever lasting life wine whispering pine.

WINERY SNOW

Wind blows all direction old man sixty winters past old man winter winery snow.
Gaze snow capped mountain prairie white day night glow winery snow.
Snow ball fight man built snow top hat eyes char coaled glow winery snow.
Older time ice cream made of snow snowy white flakes sent above pastures white
grazing buck doe winery snow.

WILD FLOWER

Grass morning dew diamond enshrined beauty heart not cower wild flower.

Mortal flesh enchanted morning fog fragrance serene still nature's beauty power wild flower.

Rose silk majestic beauty early dawn free temptation insensitive heart resentment things sour wild flower.

Come dine table peace for ever hold drink of my cup flower hold sleep tower wild flower.

WHY ME

Life society lump throat eye see question why me.
Fellow man helping hand humble be why me.
Reach one not comprehend inner wisdom kneel why me.
Heart without reason hope pine lost decree why me.

ABOUT THE AUTHOR

KING IVES
Place Of Birth: Greeley-Ville, S.C.
Residence: Kingstree, S.C.
Father: Merit Ives
Mother: Melba Arid Ives
Sister: Marie Ives-Sacramento California (Deceased)
Sister: Carolyn Ives Brown-Manning, S.C.
Brother: William J. Ives-Columbus, N.C.
School: Greeley Ville High School
Education: Graduate Greeley Ville High School
Religion: Puente Costal Holiness
Sport: Track School Record Half Mile (880) 2:05.6
Hobbies: Horse Back Riding And Gardening

Printed in the United States
By Bookmasters